ABOUT IRWIN PROFESSIONAL PUBLISHING

Irwin Professional Publishing is the nation's premier publisher of business books. As a Times Mirror company, we work closely with Times Mirror training organizations, including Zenger-Miller, Inc., Learning International, Inc., and Kaset International, to serve the training needs of business and industry.

About the Business Skills Express Series

This expanding series of authoritative, concise, and fast-paced books delivers high-quality training on key business topics at a remarkably affordable cost. The series will help managers, supervisors, and frontline personnel in organizations of all sizes and types hone their business skills while enhancing job performance and career satisfaction.

Business Skills Express books are ideal for employee seminars, independent self-study, on-the-job training, and classroom-based instruction. Express books are also convenient-to-use references at work.

CONTENTS

Self-Assessment

This self-assessment will highlight areas you may want to concentrate on in approaching situations that require corrective or disciplinary action. Respond to the 10 statements below by circling T or F.

T F **1.** Blatant or deliberate violation of company policies requires a manager to take immediate corrective action.

T F **2.** Employees continue disruptive behavior if they see no reason to change.

T F **3.** Formal written warnings have little or no impact on most employee behaviors.

T F **4.** Formal disciplinary action is usually the first step in dealing with employees who create problems.

T F **5.** Timing a corrective discussion means selecting a time when the employee is most receptive to discussion.

T F **6.** Company practices offer pointers on how to handle a specific situation.

T F **7.** Terminating an employee is the end result of the disciplinary process.

T F **8.** Careful documentation can help prevent future discrimination charges.

T F **9.** It is useful to let an employee cool down before engaging in discussion about behavior.

T F **10.** Usually a written warning will resolve the employee situation and further monitoring will not be required.

Answers to Self-Assessment

Check your responses with these listed below.

T   **1.** Blatant or deliberate violation of company policies needs immediate corrective action to prevent the occurrence of more serious problems.

T   **2.** Employees will continue disruptive behavior if they see no reason to change or receive no reward for acting otherwise.

F   **3.** Formal written warnings often have an immediate impact on employee behavior and can turn around a difficult situation.

F   **4.** Informal corrective discussions are usually the first step in dealing with employees who create problems.

F   **5.** Timing a corrective discussion means talking to the employee as close to the event/problem as possible so that it is still fresh in the employee's mind.

T   **6.** It is important to understand how a company has handled similar situations in the past and to follow company guidelines.

F   **7.** Terminating an employee occurs when the process has failed.

T   **8.** Careful documentation can help prevent future discrimination charges.

T   **9.** Emotionally charged employees have difficulty in discussing the problems and in creating solutions.

F   **10.** All situations require monitoring and follow-up in order to actually resolve the problem.

Guidelines to answering these questions and more are covered in *Supervising the Difficult Employee*. Good luck in your practice and in refining your new skills!

1 | The Difficult Situation

This chapter will help you to:

- Identify situations that require immediate management response.
- Respond to the difficult employee using the Four Action Keys.

---

dif·fi·cult (dif′i kelt, -kult′) adj. [ME., back-formation ff.] 1. hard to do, make, manage, understand, etc.; involving trouble or requiring extra effort, skill, or thought.

Webster's New World Dictionary

Words Said in Anger—Part 1

Ron Filiault, a customer service department manager, is interrupted by one of his senior processors. "Ron, you have to come up to the department right now. Lil and Marguerite are shouting at each other. It's unbelievable!" Ron leaves his lunch and hurries up the flight of stairs. He cannot imagine that these two women—both about fifty, and one a grandmother—could be fighting. Lil has been with the department less than a year and has proved to be highly efficient and competent. Marguerite, a three-year employee (though less competent), has handled all the routine duties acceptably. As Ron enters, Lil shouts at Marguerite, "I'm sick of you whistling to your-self while I work!" The two women are standing and glaring at each other across their abutting desks. ■

1

■ Q u e s t i o n s   t o   C o n s i d e r

If you were Ron, what would you do first?

_____

_____

In your judgment, how serious is a situation in which two coworkers publicly confront each other and shout at each other?

_____

_____

What is your company policy (written or unwritten) on employee fighting?

_____

_____

_____

COMMON PROBLEMS

At one time or another, you will be faced with managing difficult employee situations. Confronting and correcting these situations will require you to take extra effort and demonstrate effective evaluation and persuasion skills. You will need to know your company policy, and you will need to have practice in each of these situations so that you can fairly and accurately administer those policies.

Common employee problems that require correction/redress include:

Frequent, unexcused absenteeism.

Abrasive or threatening behavior.

Theft of company property.

Continued violation of company policies.

Excessive personal telephone calls.

Unauthorized use of company equipment.

Abuse of company credit cards.

Wasting or damaging materials.

Reckless or hazardous behavior.

Drinking on the job.

Disrupting the work of others with gossip and rumors.

Walking off the job.

The challenge of managing the difficult employee situation is first to identify the root of the problem, and then to provide effective direction to the employee who must correct the problem or change the behavior. As you'll see in this book, these skills *can* be learned and refined. Like any other skills, practice leads to success.

Words Said in Anger—Part 2

Ron found that asking both women to step into his office was a mistake. Their angry feelings continued to burst forth and he could not conduct a rational conversation. He asked that each take some time to compose herself and that he would meet with each of them separately. Lil went to lunch and Marguerite went to the ladies' room. During the individual interviews, Ron discovered that each was bothered by the work habits or idiosyncrasies of the other. Lil "threw work across the desk, talked loudly and offensively," and generally intimidated Marguerite. Marguerite, on the other hand, was "slow and inaccurate, talked and whistled to herself, and chit-chatted instead of getting the job done." Ron found that both women were concerned about rumors that the company might lay off employees and that their jobs might be eliminated. ∎

Questions to Consider

After getting the employees' individual perspectives, what should Ron do to resolve the employee differences?

_____

_____

_____

This public altercation may have an impact on coworkers. What, if anything, should Ron do or say in respect to the other department employees?

_____

_____

_____

Should Ron take any formal action, such as issuing written warnings or suspending the employees without pay, or should he wait and see if the two women can resolve their differences?

_____

_____

_____

Ron refers to a page in his personnel policy manual. (This list also appears in the employee handbook that each employee receives upon hire.):

Employees are expected to observe all policies and to act in an honest and responsible manner. The following examples of inappropriate behavior may be causes for disciplinary action, up to and including termination of employment:

1. Unauthorized disclosure of confidential company or employee information.
2. Possession, use, and/or working under the influence of alcohol on company premises.
3. Possession, distribution, or sale of illegal drugs.
4. Falsification of company, customer, or employee records.
5. Theft of company or employee property.
6. Intentional destruction of company or employee property.
7. Changing or defacing any time card.
8. Excessive absenteeism or tardiness.
9. Fighting or instigating acts of violence.
10. Walking off the job.
11. Bringing weapons of any kind onto company premises.
12. Insubordination, or refusal to follow a manager's instruction.

The above list is not meant to be an exhaustive list but to provide examples of unacceptable behavior and policy violations.

Words Said in Anger—Part 3

Three days after the altercation, Ron conducts a joint meeting with Lil and Marguerite. At the meeting, they discuss the reasons for the strain in their personal relationship and outline steps to work productively together. The steps include separating overlapping job duties, moving their desks apart, and treating each other with understanding and respect. Ron clarifies their duties and wants to meet with them together in one week to see if all the issues have been addressed. Both women assure him that everything will be resolved and that they will not be the cause of any department disruption again.

Before the second meeting with his two employees Ron decides that he will put both of the women on 60 days' probation and that he will put a summary of the incident in their individual files. In concluding the memos for their files, Ron states:

For a period of sixty days I expect:

1. That Lil/Marguerite will not engage in any disruptive conversations or altercations while at work.
2. That each will perform all the duties of their assigned tasks diligently and without comment about how the other is working.
3. That each will keep any personal differences to themselves and will work cooperatively.

If these objectives are not met at any time during the sixty-day period, I will pursue steps for termination of the employment of either or both. The essential problems are not management problems and must be resolved by the employees.

■ Questions to Consider

Do you agree with Ron's decision to place the two employees on probation? Why or why not?

_____

_____

_____

_____

How do you think Lil and Marguerite will react to Ron's notice that they are on sixty days' probation?

_____

_____

_____

_____

If the essential problem is an employee issue, what is Ron's role in ensuring that employees will be successful in their efforts?

_____

_____

_____

_____

Why is it in Ron's interest to see that the employees are successful?

_____

_____

_____

_____

Words Said in Anger—Resolution

When Ron meets again with Lil and Marguerite, he begins the meeting by emphasizing the seriousness of their past altercation and the impact that such negative behavior has on the department. Lil agrees and tells him that both she and Marguerite are now more conscious of working together in harmony. Marguerite says that simply facing away from each other as they work has resolved many of the personality issues. Ron commends them on their progress and then concludes, "But I cannot stress enough the seriousness of this disturbance. I have thought this over and decided to put you both on sixty days' probation and place a memo in your files." He hands them each a copy of the memo to read.

Lil reacts by saying, "Ron, we really are all right now. Don't you believe that we can work together? After all, we are grownups and we admit we made a mistake." ∎

Questions to Consider

What would you say in response to Lil's protest?

_____

_____

_____

_____

Aside from ensuring that employees agree to mend their ways, why is it necessary to document disciplinary actions?

_____

_____

_____

_____

1

IDENTIFICATION: THE CRITICAL FIRST STEP

The altercation between Lil and Marguerite disrupted the department, impaired the work process, and increased personal tension. Not all problems that you face will be as clearly defined as this one. Identifying the type of problem determines the type of action you will take. After you identify the problem, you'll choose one of the following actions.

Take Immediate Corrective Action for:

- Blatant or deliberate violation of company policies.
- Threats to the well-being and safety of others.
- Deterioration of individual/group performance due to disruptive or unproductive behavior.
- Onset of negative behavior patterns that, if continued, will create adverse conditions.

Take Immediate Training Action for:

- Lack of competence in performing job duties.
- Lack of skill in performing new procedures or tasks.
- Lack of practice in using equipment or procedures.
- Lack of job results from initial training.

Take No Action for:

- Single occurrence of problem that has no significant consequences to self, others, or company.
- Personal pet peeve with no relevance to workplace.
- Self-correcting situation.
- Personal discomfort due to one's own bias.

This book focuses on taking *corrective* actions. Corrective action for employee competence, personal bias, or nonsignificant work issues is inappropriate and nonproductive. Employees who lack skill or competence are not guilty of wrongdoing. Employees who do not conform to your personal ideals may be disappointing but are not necessarily wrong or disruptive, and therefore they don't need to be corrected in a formal way.

Corrective action keeps employees moving in the right direction, enables them to be successful and productive, and protects them from unwise or unsafe activities.

Take Action

Read the following scenarios, then select and underline the appropriate management action. The first one is completed for you.

1. Your work group has received the first new circuits to weld. One of your longer-term employees is having difficulty with the welding procedure.

    Corrective Action   <u>Training Action</u>   No Action

2. One of your employees sells cosmetics during lunch. Today she has been making deliveries all morning in between processing her regular work.

    Corrective Action   Training Action   No Action

3. The morning receptionist reported that the night security guard was asleep at his post again. She could not get in the building to open up the switchboard on time.

    Corrective Action   Training Action   No Action

4. One of your secretaries types her church bulletin at her desk during her break. This occurs once a month.

    Corrective Action   Training Action   No Action

5. One of your representatives has a beard. There is no company policy on beards but you think his appearance is a turnoff.

    Corrective Action   Training Action   No Action

6. You find that your new assistant manager, who was the best technician in your group, has difficulty working with her peers to complete an interdepartmental project.

    Corrective Action   Training Action   No Action

7. Complaints continue about one of your managers' personal hygiene. His employees want you to talk to him about his body odor.

    Corrective Action   Training Action   No Action

8. Orders have increased and you notice that one of your processors forgets to include accounting code information on some of the orders.

Corrective Action   Training Action   No Action

9. Your assistant complains to you that one of the sales representatives continually tells her dirty jokes. She has told him that she does not want to hear any more jokes but he continues to annoy her.

Corrective Action   Training Action   No Action

10. Your new employee, who has just completed his three-month probationary period, calls in sick on the busiest day of the week. This is the first time he has been out.

Corrective Action   Training Action   No Action

11. The telephone operator refuses to use the new company greeting. She says that it takes too long and there are too many calls.

Corrective Action   Training Action   No Action

12. One of your accounting clerks lost his temper and threw his adding machine on the floor. The machine was not damaged.

Corrective Action   Training Action   No Action

FOUR ACTION KEYS

For all employee problems, follow the four-step process as outlined next.

1. IDENTIFY the nature of the problem and why it is a problem.

Is the employee violating company policy?

Is the employee behaving inappropriately?

Is the employee failing to perform the job?

Why is the problem serious?

2. CLARIFY the reasons that the problem exists.

Does the employee understand that a problem exists?

Does the employee know and understand company policies?

Are there mitigating circumstances that affect the employee?

What is the employee's perspective?

1

3. DIRECT your employee so that the employee can correct the problem.

Ask the employee for ideas on solving the problem.

Offer your suggestions for correcting the problem.

Give specific examples or guidelines for the employee to follow.

Agree on the solutions.

4. SUPPORT your employee's efforts to correct the problem.

Thank the employee for being willing to correct the problem.

Encourage the employee to continue his or her problem-solving efforts.

Provide direction if the employee loses confidence.

Applaud the employee's success in resolving the issue.

These Four Action Keys are essential to changing employee behavior rather than merely temporarily redirecting it. Remember that lasting, long-term change is a major goal of managing difficult employees.

Prepare for managing your next difficult employee situation by completing the Four Action Keys Sheet.

FOUR ACTION KEYS SHEET

Employee name _____ Date _____

IDENTIFY
I identify the problem as _____

_____

_____

_____

This is a problem because _____

_____

_____

1

FOUR ACTION KEYS SHEET (concluded)

CLARIFY
I will verify my employee's understanding by _____
_____
_____

I will use the following as illustrations of the problem _____
_____
_____
_____
_____

DIRECT
I will prompt my employee for ideas by _____
_____
_____

My suggestions may include _____
_____
_____
_____

This situation may require disciplinary action because _____
_____
_____

SUPPORT
I can encourage my employee by _____
_____
_____

I will follow up by _____
_____
_____

Think about It

1. Identify a difficult situation with one of your employees.

   _____

   _____

   _____

2. What do you think is your employee's perspective of the difficult problem you identified?

   _____

   _____

   _____

3. What are your company's policies and practices for handling this type of violation or infraction?

   _____

   _____

   _____

4. Can you describe your plan for disciplinary action?

   _____

   _____

   _____

1

Tips

Employee handbooks detail company rules and policies and often describe expected behavior such as "friendly customer service" or "treat all team members with courtesy and respect."

If you *identify* your employee's problem as a rule violation, remind your employee of the statement in the employee handbook. *Clarify* any aspect of the rules that your employee does not understand.

Direct all your employees to refer to their handbooks on a regular basis. Occasionally, conduct a refresher meeting where employees can discuss company policies.

Support employee efforts to abide by company rules and to conduct themselves professionally, by actively recognizing employee actions.

Chapter 1 Checkpoints

✓ Do not let employees' personal conflicts prevent you from taking corrective action.

✓ Use your personnel policies to clarify rules for employees.

✓ Support your employees' efforts in the correction process.

2 | A Five-Step Correction Plan

This chapter will help you to:

- Identify the causes of employee nonperformance and noncompliance.
- Conduct a corrective discussion with an employee using the Five-Step Process.
- Describe the impact of problem behavior.

Absent without Merit

Tom Zheng left his performance appraisal interview in shock. His new supervisor was withholding his merit increase until he improved his attendance record. If he maintained a perfect record for the next several months, he might receive an increase. Tom decided to talk to Milt O'Connell, the print shop manager, who supervised his work on special projects and had made some favorable comments on his review.

Milt:

   I can understand why you're disappointed, Tom. But according to Maria you were absent 23 times last year.

Tom:

   When John was the boss, he didn't seem to care if I was out. I did a great job. I don't see why I shouldn't get a raise.

Milt:

   Did John speak to you about being out a lot?

2

Tom:

He mentioned it once, after Maria was hired to train for the supervisor spot. And, to tell you the truth, I didn't know I was out so much. John never said anything about that. I was John's best worker.

Milt:

Well, I know that you are a great worker. But the mail room is a busy place. I don't think there are enough people in there to keep up with the work as it is—it's tough on everyone else when you're out.

Tom:

I understand that. Maria talked to me about that, too. But I can't help it if I'm accident prone. I didn't plan to be in two car accidents two weekends in a row! John was a lot more understanding than Maria.

Milt:

Well, Maria is in charge now. And you guys have a ton of work. It isn't going to get any slower in there.

Tom:

But, Milt, you know I do a great job when I'm there. I don't take breaks, I don't make mistakes, I work hard!

Milt:

Key point, Tom: *when you're there* . . . Think about it.

Tom:

Yeah . . . yeah. ■

█ Probable Cause

Complete the numbered statement by circling the answers that you think apply to Tom's situation.

THE EMPLOYEE

1. Tom's excessive absenteeism is a result of

   a. His deliberate maliciousness.
   b. Failure of his supervisor to point out the problem.
   c. Circumstances over which he has no control.
   d. His lack of understanding about company rules.
   e. His boredom with the job.
   f. Failure of his supervisor to emphasize the importance of attendance.
   g. His perception of reward for good performance.

THE SUPERVISORS

2. John, Tom's first supervisor, may have not spoken to Tom about his absenteeism because he

   a. Did not want to upset Tom.
   b. Did not pay attention to his employees' absences.
   c. Did not think it was important.
   d. Considered Tom a superior performer and overlooked his absences.
   e. Had attendance problems of his own.
   f. Did not know what to do.
   g. Was saving the discussion for the annual performance appraisal.

3. Maria, Tom's current supervisor, has taken action because

   a. Tom's attendance affects the department's ability to get its job done.
   b. She does not like Tom and wants to make an example.
   c. Tom is violating the company policy on attendance.
   d. John did a poor job supervising the department.
   e. Others in the department may also become lax in their attendance at work.

f. She wants Tom to take his job and the company rules seriously.

g. She is sick of working overtime when employees are out.

As you can see, there are two sides to every difficult situation, the employee's and the supervisor's. Let's take a look at both prespectives.

THE EMPLOYEE'S PERSPECTIVE

Employees perform their best when they have reasons and rewards. In the previous scenario, Tom did not clearly understand that his pattern of absences created a negative impact on his personal overall performance (no merit increase), on his department coworkers (more work and overtime), and on his new supervisor (disciplinary action). Because Tom was not informed that his absenteeism was excessive, he may have felt that taking time out was a reward for his performance. Or, he may have understood that his attendance was not good, but his supervisor looked the other way because he was a favored worker.

On the other hand, Tom may have felt he had neither reason nor reward to come to work every day. He may not have felt that his contribution was valued by his supervisor. He may have felt that the work was unimportant and that the pay was not equal to his effort.

■ **Your Turn**

In your experience, what are typical reasons employees do not act or perform in the way you want them to?

_____

_____

_____

What rewards would motivate employees to act or perform in the most effective ways?

_____

_____

_____

THE SUPERVISOR'S PERSPECTIVE

Supervisors are accountable for directing and motivating their employees.

In the case of Tom Zheng, John and Maria have a responsibility to ensure that their employees complete work to company standards, adhere to company policies, and achieve their highest individual levels of performance.

Communicating to Tom the importance of attendance, the impact his absence creates on the rest of the department, and the value placed on Tom's individual contribution may have prevented the need for disciplinary action. Early communication would have given Tom the opportunity to correct his actions and improve his overall performance.

Allowing an employee's negative behavior to continue for an extended period of time can infect other employees with similar habits or behaviors. Morale of the work unit can deteriorate; then output suffers. Left unattended, the problem spreads, and the supervisor is confronted with more complicated problems.

Fear is the single most quoted reason that supervisors fail to take immediate action on a difficult situation. Supervisors fear the reactions of their employees. Supervisors fear that they lack the competence to deal with the interpersonal situation. Supervisors fear that they will do the wrong thing and make the situation worse.

Reconsider the problem you identified in Chapter 1. What are your fears? How do you plan to deal with them?

_____

_____

_____

_____

2

THE CORRECTIVE DISCUSSION

An effective discussion can be broken into five steps. When you want to correct employee performance or behavior, use the Five-Step Process to get results.

1. **Select** the appropriate time and space to discuss the issues that concern you.
   a. Time your discussion as close to the occurrence as possible so that your employee clearly recognizes the event.
   b. Make sure that your discussion is private and free from interruptions.

2. **State** in concise terms the event, actions, and behavior, and the reason for your concerns.
   a. Describe specifically, using supporting facts.
   b. Tell your employee why you are concerned.
   c. Describe the impact of the employee's actions.

3. **Solicit** the employee's perspective.
   a. Listen to your employee's reasons, perceptions, and feelings.
   b. Keep your employee focused on the specific event.

4. **Seek** solutions and employee commitment.
   a. Prod your employee for realistic solutions. If your employee cannot think of any, make suggestions.
   b. Press for employee commitment to the solutions. Refer to the impact of the action or behavior.

5. **Support** the employee's resolutions.
   a. Reinforce your employee's strengths and ability to make the needed changes.
   b. Recognize your employee's change or improvement within thirty days of your discussion.

The next case study shows the Five-Step Process in action. Joann Stitchly, night nurse manager, has called in one of the nurses, Laura Winchell, for a discussion of Laura's behavior. Read the case study and critique Joann's discussion. Has she used the Five-Step Process effectively?

Patient Professional Preferred

Laura:

You wanted to see me?

Joann:

Yes, please step in here so we won't be interrupted (indicates a small conference room). I have something I'd like to discuss with you privately.

Laura:

What is it?

Joann:

I have had some complaints recently about the way you conduct yourself with other members of the staff. I want to talk to you about the impact you are having on other employees and on patient service.

Laura:

(Stung) What? You can't be serious. I always conduct myself in a most professional manner. I consider myself to be one of the most efficient nurses on the floor.

Joann:

No one is complaining about your efficiency. It's the manner in which you conduct yourself that is a problem.

Laura:

I suppose those two featherbrains I work with have been complaining. They're always chatting or running out for smoke breaks. I really cannot believe you are singling me out because of their complaints.

Joann:

Your coworkers are professionals too, Laura. If you have a problem with the way they conduct themselves I would expect to hear from you about that. But they are not the only source of complaints. The dietary manager was upset about how you handled one of her volunteers. Last week you reprimanded a dietary aide . . .

Laura:

Well, she deserved it. She talked back. What else could I do?

Joann:

Do you think shouting at her in front of the patient was an effective way of handling the situation?

Laura:

(Pause) Perhaps it wasn't. But I was under pressure. We were short-staffed. In good conscience I could not overlook her carelessness.

Joann:

We all work under pressure. It does not give anyone—you or me—the license to speak harshly to other staff members and embarrass them in front of the patients. Last night you refused to answer Jane's question about a patient's medicine . . .

Laura:

I just assumed she knew. She was standing right there when the doctor gave the orders.

Joann:

Laura, it was her first week on the floor. She was looking to you for direction. You are the most senior person I have at night. You have the most experience. What's going on?

Laura:

I don't know, Joann. Maybe I'm just losing it.

2

Joann:

You have been working steadily for six months with no time off. But it's not like you to snap at people or refuse to help them.

Laura:

I know. I'd rather be at work than at home. It's Stacey again.

Joann:

You know, Laura, you can't let your home stress spill over and ruin your relationships here.

Laura:

I know.

Joann:

What are you going to do about it?

Laura:

I can't change my home situation, and I can't keep up these hours, obviously. I don't even like *myself*. I guess I'll take some time off.

Joann:

That may help, Laura. Some time to yourself can give you a better perspective. What are you going to do about the nurses you've alienated?

Laura:

I guess I've got to tone it down. I'm on edge and taking it out on the others. I'll apologize to Jane . . . and speak to dietary.

Joann:

That's a start. I understand how tough it is when you have trouble with Stacey. But I can't emphasize enough how important it is that we all work in harmony here. You know that we depend on each other to take care of all of our patients. And I depend on you, Laura. You're efficient. You're a real pro. You might also want to

2

consider getting some counseling for your home situation. That may help you in dealing with your stress here *and* at home.

Laura:

I hear you. I think it's time for me to take some positive action. Thanks, Joann. Sorry I caused a problem.

Joann:

It isn't one that you can't solve. You know I'm always around if you need me. And don't forget, if one of the nurses is not doing her job, let me know. That's *my* job. ■

■ Your Turn

Under each of the following Five-Step headings, evaluate Joann's performance of that step.

1. SELECT: How was the timing and location of the interview?

_____
_____
_____
_____

2. STATE: How was Joann's statement of the problem?

_____
_____
_____
_____

3. SOLICIT: How did Joann receive and react to her employee's perspective?

_____
_____
_____
_____

4. SEEK: How did Joann do at reaching a solution?

_____

_____

_____

_____

5. SUPPORT: Comment on Joann's show of support for her employee.

_____

_____

_____

_____

> **Tip** ─────────────────────────────
>
> If you observe or learn that an employee is creating problems, speak to that employee as soon as possible. The earlier the employee is alerted to the situation, the sooner it can be corrected.

PROBLEM IMPACT

As seen in Chapter 1, identifying a problem is critical. But how do you convince the difficult employee that there is a _reason_ that his or her actions are problematic and must be changed? You must be able to motivate employees to stop negative actions and to change or alter their behavior. Your employees must understand why change is essential.

In the right-hand column below, consider reasons for changing behavior. The reasons need to be convincing. Imagine that your employee just doesn't understand _why_ change is crucial. The first example is completed as a model.

2

Employee Action	Why It Is a Problem and Why Employee Must Change
Tom is absent 23 times in a twelve-month period.	Daily attendance is important for getting all the work done. When he is out so often it is unfair to everyone else. They are doing their own job plus his job.
Headwaiter fails to press his uniform. Presents a rumpled appearance.	
Accounting supervisor won't answer her own phone. Too busy.	
Clerk makes long-distance personal telephone calls during slow periods.	
Key member of a committee is constantly late to meetings. Anywhere from 10 to 30 minutes.	
Programmer does not listen to users when making changes. Too busy socializing. Doesn't take notes.	
Sales rep is terrific in dealing with customer problems but treats support staff with disrespect. Belittles and makes snide remarks.	

Employee Action	Why It Is a Problem and Why Employee Must Change
Employee gossiped with customer about company president's divorce proceedings.	
New supervisor reprimands cashier about her appearance at register with customers present.	
Receptionist in busy office eats and drinks coffee while signing in visitors.	
To create good morale, supervisor tells jokes while working side by side with men on line. This slows production down.	
Long-term employee cries every time he has to use new computer system.	

The ability to provide a rationale for change is a key strength. Often, if employees aren't convinced of the need to change, workplace problems continue leading to an ongoing and more widespread climate of discomfort. The next chapter covers what can happen when problems grow beyond the point of early identification and discussion leading to change.

Chapter 2 Checkpoints

For Successful Change

✓ Make certain that your employees know and understand your company policies.

✓ Act on early indicators that an employee needs to be redirected.

✓ Follow the Five-Step Process when correcting an employee's actions.

✓ Give your employee your vote of confidence that the problem can be corrected.

3 | Determining the Facts

This chapter will help you to: ————————————

- Determine whether disciplinary action is necessary.
- Investigate facts to support taking action.

First-Time Offender

Roy Grant has just spoken to one of his accountants about telling dirty jokes to the secretarial staff. One of the women complained to Roy and asked him to speak with Philip Salerno about it. While Roy personally thought that the two jokes were not that bad (in fact one was pretty funny), he reminded Philip that the company had a policy on harassing behavior, that what he—Philip—might think amusing was not necessarily true for others, and that this was an accounting firm, not a social club. Philip, a bit put out, agreed that he would not tell dirty jokes or make off-color remarks to the women.

Roy decides to call the personnel manager about one final item. "Hi Pat. I've just spoken to Philip and he has agreed to conduct himself more thoughtfully. I feel confident that he won't do it again. This isn't something I have to write up for his personnel file, is it?" ■

If you were the personnel manager, what would you say? _____

_____

_____

3

DECIDING ON FORMAL ACTION

A formal write-up placed in an employee's file can have a significant impact on an employee's behavior, motivation, and feelings at work. Consider four factors when determining what formal action you will take:

1. The seriousness of the offense.
2. The employee's overall performance record.
3. The employee's understanding of the situation.
4. Your company's policies and practices in similar cases.

Let's take a closer look at these factors.

Seriousness of the Offense

Ask the following questions to determine the potential seriousness of the problem.

- Is it legally actionable (e.g., selling drugs, stealing)?
- Does it create liability for the company?
- Is there potential of lawsuit or financial loss?
- Does it threaten the safety of others?
- Does it disrupt or prevent work of others?

For example, in the case we just studied, Philip's jokes were annoying and distasteful. If Philip had acted in a gross and threatening manner and had touched the female employees, do you think Roy, his manager, would call personnel and question the need to write up the account? How would Roy's reaction be different?

_____

_____

_____

Employee's Overall Record

You'll also need to take into account the employee's record at work. Consider these questions.

- Does the employee have a history of complaints?
- Does the employee have current performance problems?
- Is the employee new and without job history?
- Does the employee have a history of personal problems that affect work?
- Does the employee have attendance problems?
- Has the employee deliberately broken company rules in the past?

Consider the case in Chapter 2, concerning the nurse who had reprimanded the aide in front of a patient. What was the night nurse manager's description of Laura's past performance?

_____

_____

_____

Employee's Understanding of the Situation

Take a close look at the employee's understanding of the problem. Ask these questions to see if the employee realizes the scope of his or her actions.

- Did the employee know that what he or she was doing violated company policy?
- Did the employee recognize the negative impact on other employees, customers, or others?
- Was the employee aware of the consequences of his or her actions?
- Did the employee receive conflicting directions?

- What were the other circumstances that prompted the employee to behave as he/she did?

For example, consider the case in Chapter 1. As a manager, would you expect that both employees understood fighting to be inappropriate behavior and that serious action might be required?

_____

_____

Company Policy and Practice

Finally, consider consistent company policy. Is there a "company line" on this type of behavior?

- What has your company done in the past in similar circumstances?
- How have employees been treated for similar offenses?
- What does your policy manual state?

What does your own company list as policy violations that require disciplinary action or possible termination?

_____

_____

_____

_____

THE INCIDENT FILE

It is important to keep records of any incident that occurs. If the employee acts as agreed and changes his or her behavior, the event becomes a single incident. If, however, the employee fails to change behavior, your initial record—in the form of an incident file—becomes a critical piece in future dealings with the employee.

After speaking to the personnel manager, Roy decides to complete an incident report on Philip's behavior, and place it in his incident file. Roy believes that his discussion with his employee will take care of the problem behavior. Following is an example of the incident report that Roy completed for Philip's incident file.

3

INCIDENT REPORT

Employee(s) involved: Philip Salerno, Mary Brodsky

INCIDENT SUMMARY

Date: 05/06/93   Mary Brodsky asked to speak to me about Philip. She said that on Tuesday he stood around talking at coffee break by their desks and started telling dirty jokes. She ignored him. But on Wednesday he was back again with another joke and some off-color remarks that she found offensive and degrading. She spoke with Elaine and Marta after and they agreed with her. She did not feel comfortable addressing Philip so she came to me.

DISCUSSION WITH EMPLOYEE

Regarding: ( ) Policy violation   (X) Inappropriate behavior

DATE: 05/07/93   Told Philip I had received a complaint about his language and telling dirty jokes to the secretaries. He knew immediately what I was talking about. I told him that it was not acceptable behavior and that we expected him to refrain from that in the future.

AGREED ACTIONS

1. Philip agreed not to tell dirty jokes in front of the women.

2. He agreed to be more respectful of women.

3. He agreed to watch his language, as this could affect his career at this company.

FOLLOW-UP ACTIONS

_____

_____

_____

Complete the following incident report for one of your own employee situations.

INCIDENT REPORT

Employee(s) involved: _____

_____

INCIDENT SUMMARY

Date: /   /   _____

_____

_____

_____

_____

DISCUSSION WITH EMPLOYEE

Regarding: ( ) Policy violation   ( ) Inappropriate behavior

Date: /   /   _____

_____

_____

_____

AGREED ACTIONS

1. _____
2. _____
3. _____

FOLLOW-UP ACTIONS

_____

_____

Read the following case study and analyze how this manager determines what type of formal action to take. Answer the Questions to Consider following the case.

Gossip Detection

It has taken Luanne ten hours (seven interviews and three second interviews with the members of the claims processing unit) to uncover the source of vicious rumors that have turned the unit upside down for the past three months. Yesterday, Maureen (the unit supervisor) had come to Luanne in tears and told her that someone was spreading a rumor that she was running around with the claims manager. This rumor sounded similar to the one that had circulated the month before about one of the night supervisors. Luanne is determined to track down the rumormonger and put an end to the uproars. In every case, the rumor was injurious to one of the unit employees and work came to a standstill.

Rhonda Moore's file lies open on Luanne's desk. Luanne's interviews have traced the rumors to Rhonda, who transferred to the unit about five months ago. Luanne's notes read:

1. **Seriousness:** Unfounded malicious rumors detrimental to individuals. Complete work stoppage on two occasions.

2. **Rhonda's record:** Two years of average performance reviews. Two past reprimands—one for personal phone calls, the other for gossiping. Former supervisor was preparing another memo to file for discipline before Rhonda transferred.

3. **Rhonda's view:** Denies any involvement with rumors. Denies telling anyone anything. (Note: five employees independently stated that Rhonda had told them what she "heard." Three confirm each others' stories. Several times Rhonda spoke in group setting.)

4. Policy: Work stoppage considered serious offense. Cited in employee handbook.

Luanne decides to meet with Rhonda and confront her with evidence and a written warning. She sifts through her notes and prepares the following warning notice. ■

WARNING NOTICE

Employee name: Rhonda Moore   Date of Notice: 10/3/94

On the above date, I warned the above-named employee concerning the following: Spreading false and malicious rumors about co-workers, thereby creating serious work stoppages in the claims department. Independent interviews with employees in the unit confirmed that Rhonda deliberately made false statements about her supervisor and the claims manager and about two other department clerks and a night supervisor. These rumors were of a personal, nonbusiness nature and created uproar in the department. In two instances, other department employees accused Rhonda of spreading rumors and work stopped in the department while accusations were exchanged. The work stoppage on last Friday was brought to my attention and I conducted an investigation on Monday and Tuesday. As a result of the investigation I found that Rhonda was the primary source of rumor. As of this date, Rhonda must cease gossiping and spreading false rumors immediately.

This warning places the employee in probationary status for 90 days. The employee may not be considered for a salary increase or a job transfer/promotion while on probation. If the above incident reoccurs during the next 90 days, the result will be:

___ Second written warning
___ Suspension
XX Discharge

_____   _____
Supervisor's Signature   Date

I acknowledge that a copy of the above warning has been given to me.

_____   _____
Employee's Signature   Date

■ Questions to Consider

What were the deciding factors that prompted Luanne to give Rhonda a written warning?

_____

_____

_____

_____

3

In your opinion, how serious is Rhonda's gossiping? What are the possible consequences of continued gossiping?

_____

_____

_____

_____

In your opinion, was the consequence for Rhonda's noncompliance too severe, or fair? Why?

_____

_____

_____

CONDUCTING AN INVESTIGATION

To properly and fairly administer policy and direct employees, managers must ensure that they obtain accurate information about events, actions, and results. By following four steps, you can get the facts you need to support any disciplinary action you decide to take.

Interview

Interview employee participants and observers to get a clear understanding of the difficult situation. Ask for facts, viewpoints, and sequence of events. Dig for details and specifics. Be sure to listen impartially to all statements.

Record

Record all statements, names of contributors, and dates of interviews. Use a notebook, and maintain a list of dates and contacts. Write down the exact words used by witnesses/participants. Do not erase misstatements. Write corrections below original statements so you have an accurate record over time.

Confirm

Confirm with contributing employees all statements by reading the employees' comments and statements back to them. Ask them to clarify any details that are unclear and to verify all data that you read.

Assess

Assess the situation with all the evidence at hand. Review all facts and put them in sequential order. Note discrepancies and restatements or corrections to original statements. Put all the facts in order before drawing conclusions.

As you move through the investigation, use all your powers of observation and intuition to get at the facts of the problem you're considering. Remember that many employees won't feel comfortable informing management about their colleagues, so be sensitive to employees' privacy and also to issues of confidentiality. Use a checklist like the one that follows to evaluate the results of your investigation.

THE INVESTIGATOR'S CHECKLIST

Y N **1.** Have all parties involved been interviewed?

Y N **2.** Do dates and times correspond?

Y N **3.** Are the facts identical from each reporting party?

Y N **4.** Are there contradictory statements? Facts?

Y N **5.** Are contradictions due to lack of facts given by the person reporting?

Y N **6.** Are contradictions false statements or coverups?

Y N **7.** Do personal feelings or biases color any of the statements?

Y N **8.** Is there any confusion regarding events or facts?

Y N **9.** Are there numerous corrections to facts/statements?

Y N **10.** Are there items that people refuse to discuss?

Y N **11.** Do people who are reluctant to testify fear retaliation?

Y N **12.** Are there company obstacles that prevent people from speaking up?

Y N **13.** Have the opinions of observers been sought out?

Y N **14.** Do past employment or performance records support employee actions or reactions?

Y N **15.** Is the occurrence a variation on an employee performance problem?

3

Chapter 3 Checkpoints

✓ Investigate all difficult situations for facts and details.

✓ In recording an incident, organize the facts in a clear, concise manner.

✓ Before taking formal action, consider the seriousness of the offense and the employee's past performance record.

✓ Review company policy and procedures for guidance in handling difficult situations.

4 | Taking Progressive Action

This chapter will help you to:

- Take action when employee behavior or performance does not change.
- Follow a progressive disciplinary process.

Broken Promises

"Hey, Louis!" shouts Sam Hernandez, the shipping supervisor. "You're late!"

Louis Garcia shrugs his shoulders as he passes Sam and says, "Sorry, boss. My car wouldn't start so I had to hitch a ride with my sister who works downtown."

Sam motions Louis to stop. He taps his clipboard. "Look Louis, this is the third time I've had to speak to you this month. You know the rules around here. You have to show up on time. We have orders to get out and they won't wait for you."

"I know, I know. I promise, Sam, I'm going to get my car fixed and then I won't have any more problems." Louis gives Sam the same sincere look he has given Sam before.

Sam shakes his head. "I mean it, Louis. You're in for trouble if you don't shape up." Louis nods and turns to hang his jacket on a nearby hook. ■

■ Questions to Consider

Louis does not appear to take Sam's warning seriously. What should Sam do now?

_____

_____

_____

_____

What are valid reasons for arriving at work on time?

_____

_____

_____

_____

How can Sam motivate Louis to get to work on time?

_____

_____

_____

_____

THE DISCIPLINARY PROCESS

If you are faced with employees who continually ignore your directions or fail to take correctional discussions, work commitments, and work rules seriously, you need to implement a formal disciplinary process. The purpose of the process is to correct the situation. The following descriptions will help you select the most appropriate action to take when you are confronted with a disciplinary situation.

Step One: The Oral Warning.   The oral warning calls an employee's attention to behavior, performance, or a situation that needs immediate improvement and correction. Use it when:

Employee does not change after correctional discussion.

Violation is a minor infraction of standard company policy.

Minor loss or injury is involved.

Actions to Take

- Restate the problem that needs correction.
- Indicate that you are giving the employee an oral warning, which will be placed in the employee's personnel file.
- Complete a summary memo for the personnel file.

In the chapter's opening example, Sam Hernandez can use an oral warning to emphasize the importance of correcting tardiness. Sam's oral warning memo would be placed in Louis's personnel file.

4

Memo to File of Louis Garcia
From: Sam Hernandez, Supervisor
Date: October 22, 1993

Oral Warning

Today I spoke to Louis Garcia about his tardiness. Louis had been late three times this month. Each time he said he had car problems. I told him that our shipments had to get out on time. When he was late it made problems for the others as they are responsible for his work getting done.

He agreed to be on time from now on. I told him I was putting an oral warning in his file because he did not seem serious about correcting the problem. He said he will get his car fixed and be on time.

Step Two: The Written Warning. The written warning alerts the employee to the consequences if there is no change in behavior, performance, or a situation. Use it when:

Employee does not respond to oral warning with immediate changes.

Violation is major infraction of company policy.

Serious loss or injury is involved.

Actions to Take
- Review oral warning *or* restate company policy.
- Indicate that it is a written warning.
- Describe factually the events, your expectations, and subsequent disciplinary action if no improvement or correction occurs.
- Complete a detailed written warning. Both you and your employee should sign the warning.

If Louis did not heed the oral warning that Sam Hernandez put in his file, Sam may want to use a written warning to correct the problem. The following example shows the format and content of a typical written warning that is placed in the employee's file.

Memo to File of Louis Garcia
From: Sam Hernandez, Supervisor
Date: November 22, 1993

Written Warning

Summary
Louis Garcia received an oral warning about his tardiness on October 22. He had agreed to correct the problem and be on time. He understood that being on time was important to our department to get the shipments out on time each day. Louis was on time for the last week in October and first two weeks in November.

Incidents
This week Louis was late on Monday by 15 minutes, Tuesday by 20 minutes, and Wednesday by 45 minutes. This is unacceptable and cannot continue.

Action
Louis must report to work on time every day. If Louis does not heed this written warning he may be terminated for his tardiness.

_____   _____
Supervisor's Signature   Date

I acknowledge that I have been warned and may lose my job if I do not follow company policy.

_____   _____
Employee's Signature   Date

Alternate Step: Suspension. Suspension removes the employee from the work site for extreme behavior, usually without pay. Use it when:

Employee is violent or dangerous to him/herself and others.

Serious infraction requires investigation that may lead to termination.

Employee fails to heed one or more written warnings.

Actions to Take

- Describe the reasons that you have decided to suspend the employee.

- Describe the seriousness of the situation and the possible outcomes.
- Prepare a memo describing in detail the reasons for the suspension.
- Sign and have employee sign the memo.

Termination.   Termination is not part of the disciplinary process. It occurs when the process fails to correct the situation.

Tip ─────────────────────────────

If an employee refuses to sign the memo to acknowledge that he/she has been formally warned, ask a third party to witness the refusal and to sign the document.

What Would You Do?

Read the following scenarios. Circle the appropriate action step to determine the action you would take.

1. Last week you thoroughly explained the new check-cashing policy to all of your cashiers. You gave them copies of the guidelines to put on their registers. Your assistant manager now hands you a check that Laurie Wilson cashed. The signature is forged. Laurie, a two year veteran, did not follow the new guidelines. You decide to give:

ORAL WARNING   WRITTEN WARNING   SUSPENSION

because you feel that _____

_____

_____

2. You are the new supervisor of a 10-person unit. As you review attendance records you discover that two of the employees have attendance issues. One is out consistently two days per month; the other is sick the day before all long holiday weekends. You decide to give:

ORAL WARNING   WRITTEN WARNING   SUSPENSION

because you feel that _____

_____

_____

3. You are pretty certain that the reports about the third-shift computer operator are true. Five PCs and some VCR equipment have been stolen from the training room. Your investigation indicates that the equipment was there at the 2:00 AM security check. Only two people had access: the third-shift operator, and the security guard, who is a frail retiree. You decide to give:

ORAL WARNING   WRITTEN WARNING   SUSPENSION

because you feel that _____

_____

_____

4. The new technician is waiting to see you. Because he was chatting with a nurse this morning, he failed to give complete attention to his patient, who fell while trying to get up on the table. The patient bruised her hip and became hysterical. You decide to give:

ORAL WARNING   WRITTEN WARNING   SUSPENSION

because you feel that _____

_____

_____

5. After a stern warning on her performance appraisal, you expected your accounting supervisor to take pains not to reprimand her employees in front of others. Today, as you were coming out of the conference room, you heard her stop the accounts payable clerk in the busy office lobby and forcibly complain about the clerk's errors on the last payables run. Her last words were "Shape up Simpson or you're gone!" You decide to give:

ORAL WARNING   WRITTEN WARNING   SUSPENSION

because you feel that _____
_____
_____

6. You manage a three-person office. The receptionist and the customer service clerk do not speak to each other. The atmosphere is so tense that your clients comment on the strange behavior of your two employees. You decide to give:

ORAL WARNING   WRITTEN WARNING   SUSPENSION

because you feel that _____
_____
_____

7. You have just discovered that one of your employees has a gun and has been showing it to others on coffee break. You decide to give:

ORAL WARNING   WRITTEN WARNING   SUSPENSION

because you feel that _____
_____
_____

8. One of your marketing representatives had requested two days off before the long weekend. You are not able to grant the time off. The rep calls in sick and is out for those two days. When you call the house, his wife answers and says he has gone to Las Vegas for the weekend. You decide to give:

ORAL WARNING   WRITTEN WARNING   SUSPENSION

because you feel that _____
_____
_____

9. After work, two of your employees had a fist fight in the parking lot. Today one of the two called in sick; the other reported in and is acting extremely surly to his coworkers. You decide to give:

ORAL WARNING   WRITTEN WARNING   SUSPENSION

because you feel that _____

_____

_____

10. In reviewing Mary's file, you find that you gave her an oral warning three months ago for attendance. It seems that she is starting the same pattern all over again. This is the third time in 10 days that she has called in sick. You decide to give:

ORAL WARNING   WRITTEN WARNING   SUSPENSION

because you feel that _____

_____

_____

4

■ Time Out

Now that you know more about the disciplinary process, take a moment to evaluate your present responses to managing difficult employees. For each statement, circle the answer that best describes what you do now.

1. I learn about employee problem situations through

   a. Observing their behavior.
   b. Reports from other supervisors.
   c. Reports from other employees.

2. I respond to employee problem situations if

   a. The employee is breaking policies.
   b. The employee has a record of past problems.
   c. My supervisor asks me to speak to the employee.

3. I determine the type of disciplinary action to take after

   a. I review company policy and practice.
   b. The employee repeats the behavior or mistake four times.
   c. I see how the employee reacts to correction.

4

4. I speak to an employee regarding inappropriate behavior
   a. As close to the occurrence as possible.
   b. Within the quarter.
   c. At the annual review.

5. When discussing the employee's problem behavior I
   a. Select a private spot where we cannot be overheard.
   b. Speak quietly to the employee wherever he/she happens to be.
   c. Do it in full view of other employees.

6. In monitoring employee progress I
   a. Make a note on my calendar and make certain to speak with the employee within a specific time frame.
   b. Observe and speak to the employee only if he/she repeats the problem.
   c. Rely on the employee to keep his/her word and do not follow up with a meeting.

STRAIGHT A'S

If you have circled *a* as your typical response to managing difficult employee situations, then you understand the importance of:

1. *Observing your employees' performance, interactions with others, and personal reactions to situations.* You can quickly tell if something is amiss, if the employee is off track, or if the employee needs some assistance or guidance.

2. *Ensuring that all employees conform to policies.* Company policies are for everyone. Policies ensure a safe, pleasant, and productive working environment.

3. *Knowing and understanding your company policy for handling employee disciplinary situations.* Company guidelines ensure that all employees are treated fairly. You protect yourself and your company by following procedures.

4. *Speaking to an employee while the incident is still fresh in his/her mind.* In this way the employee readily identifies the situation, the words, the actions, or reactions that you are describing.

5. *Privacy in correcting a problem situation.* You can address the employee without embarrassing him/her in front of peers or customers. You are more likely to get more response from the employee and a commitment to action.

6. *Speaking to the employee after the discussion to ensure that the employee is back on track.* You know that an employee needs encouragement to continue the good work, or needs refocusing if he/she still is having difficulties.

4

These are all skills that grow from an understanding of the disciplinary process. The next chapter covers the process of clearly documenting the process.

Chapter 4 Checkpoints

✓ Use a progressive disciplinary process if corrective discussions fail to motivate your employee.

✓ An oral warning is a formal memo put in an employee file citing the infraction or violation.

✓ A written warning describes consequences if an employee fails to correct the situation or follow policy.

✓ A suspension is used to remove an employee from the workplace for the most serious infractions or for sensitive investigations.

5 | Writing Concise Documentation

This chapter will help you to:

- Follow eight rules for documentation.
- Write clear, concise documentation.
- Identify important and relevant data.

Managers' Round Table

At the monthly management meeting several managers discuss the ramifications of not having documentation:

Jolene:

I don't understand why the unemployment examiner did not accept the fact that my speaking to Ruth *was* a warning to her that she would lose her job.

Jon:

But I've told you before. If it isn't written down, it didn't happen.

Lucia:

Examiners have to make sure that the employees understand that their jobs are in jeopardy. Did you actually say to Ruth that if she made one more personal purchase on the company credit card she would lose her job?

Jolene:

Well, not in those words. But I certainly implied it. I mean, it was outrageous! She was purchasing her Christmas gifts with the card.

5

Martin:

Hey, she thought it was all right. After all, she paid us right back. Besides, she did it last year and no one said anything.

Jolene:

The nerve!

Lucia:

That was a good part of the problem. Last year we discovered people besides Ruth charging personal items to company credit cards. So we wrote the policy. Did you show the examiner the memo?

Jolene:

Yes. Ruth said she never saw the memo. So we got back to, "Did you put it in writing?"

Jon:

All of the details have to be in writing. Not only for outside examiners but for employees like Ruth. Sometimes when you put it in a memo and put the memo in the file, the employee takes what you say seriously and actually does what you say!

Lucia:

Jon's right. It wasn't until I put Patty on written warning that she stopped coming in late. She just didn't think that being on time was important. When I wrote it out and she realized she was hurting her job security she turned right around.

Jolene:

I just don't write well. I wouldn't know what to say.

Jon:

There are eight things that you have to remember. ■

EIGHT DOCUMENTATION RULES

Good managers know that clear documentation is crucial to successful disciplinary action. Disciplinary problems are best documented by following these important steps:

1. Identify the reason for taking disciplinary action.
2. State the nature of the disciplinary action.
3. Describe the specific offense and cause for this action.
4. Use specific facts (date, names, events) to describe the situation.
5. Use clear, concise language that is easily understood by the employee.
6. Avoid subjective statements and discriminatory remarks.
7. Do not exaggerate events or reactions.
8. Indicate the consequences of repeat offenses.

By applying these eight rules to Jolene's situation, her peers offer the following advice.

1. Identify the reason for taking disciplinary action.

   Jon:

   > Let Ruth know that she is violating a new policy.

2. State the nature of the disciplinary action.

   Lucia:

   > If it was the first time you spoke to her you could make it an oral warning. If you think she was deliberately ignoring the policy, make it written.

3. Describe the specific offense and cause for this action.

   Jolene:

   > Should I refer to what she did last year?

Jon:

No. Stick to this year's problem. Last year no one was enforcing any rules.

4. Use specific facts (date, names, events) to describe the situation.

Lucia:

Actually, that's the easy part. You say that Ruth charged four items on November 22 with the company credit card. The purchases were personal gifts and not company purchases.

5. Use clear, concise language that is easily understood by the employee.

Jolene:

I don't really write very well.

Martin:

Write like you are speaking to Ruth. You don't need to be a lawyer and use "legalese."

6. Avoid subjective statements and discriminatory remarks.

Jolene:

Could I comment on what a pill Ruth was to work with and how she took forever to get things done and that she was an old dog who refused to learn new tricks?

Lucia:

No way! Stick to the facts—not your negative opinions. And never make remarks about age, sex, race, or anything else that could be considered discriminatory.

7. Do not exaggerate events or reactions.

Jolene:

Well, she was so slow! All my people thought so.

Martin:

Not everybody. She always met deadlines and she was very accurate. You cannot exaggerate when you describe your employee in the documentation. It serves no purpose.

8. Indicate the consequences of repeat offenses.

Jolene:

How does describing what she did prevent her from doing it again?

Jon:

You conclude your memo with what will happen if Ruth continues to charge on the company card.

Lucia:

Depending on how serious you thought it was, you might say she would get another written warning. In this case, you would say that she would lose her job if she did it again. ■

PRACTICE MAKES PERFECT

Based on the memo below, analyze Stewart's documentation techniques.

MEMO

TO: Nolan Lahler
FROM: Stewart Finkel
RE: ORAL WARNING

You violated the company policy about smoking. You are not supposed to smoke in any part of the building. You may be a 25-year employee but that does not mean you get special privileges. Make sure that you do not smoke in the building again.

Of the eight documentation rules, which ones does this memo follow?

_____

_____

_____

What is the memo missing?

_____

_____

_____

_____

What effect will this memo have on the employee?

_____

_____

_____

Next, read the warning notice on page 61, bearing in mind the eight documentation rules.

WARNING NOTICE

Employee: Warren Matlock   Notice Date: 3/3/94

Reason for Warning: Policy Violation

Type of Warning: First Written Warning

On the above date, I warned the above-named employee concerning his violating a company policy by reporting to work under the influence of alcohol.

Warren went to the Hillside Cafe where he had three beers at lunch on Tuesday, March 2. When he reported to work at one o'clock, Tom Marcos, the assistant manager, noticed that Warren was walking very unsteadily and was having difficulty with hand—eye coordination. Warren admitted to Tom that he had some beers at lunch. Tom sent Warren home because he was unable to perform his job safely.

I told Warren that it was against company policy (as stated in the handbook) to come to work under the influence of alcohol—including beer. He understands that he should not have beers at lunch and that he jeopardizes himself and others.

If Warren reports to work again under the influence of alcohol, he will be suspended without pay for three days.

_____   _____
Supervisor' s Signature   Date

_____   _____
Employee's Signature   Date

How do the eight rules apply to this warning notice? Determine if the notice met all the eight criteria. Comment on what you would have written differently.

1. Reason _____

_____

2. Nature of warning _____

3. Specific offense _____

_____

_____

4. Specific facts _____
_____
_____

5. Was it clear and concise? _____

6. Was it free of subjective remarks? _____

7. Was it free of exaggeration? _____

8. Consequences _____
_____
_____

What I would have written differently
_____
_____
_____

Now consider the case of Marjorie, an order processor with three years of experience. You witness the following scenario:

Yes sir. We will get that right out to you. Thank you for your order. (Pause and tap on switchhook.)

Are you still there, Susan? . . . Good, I thought I lost you. Where was I? Oh yes, I think I'll wear my black pants, so can I borrow your red sweater? Yes, the one with . . . oh, hang on, another customer.

Good afternoon, this is Marjorie speaking. How can I help you today? Yes, and what catalog are you ordering from? I see . . . Can you hold please?

(Taps again.) Susan, I have to go. This is going to be a long one. I'll call you back after I'm through. Thanks.

Yes, ma'am. Now I have the catalog. Please, may I have your name . . . ■

5

When you look through Marjorie's personnel file, you find this memo:

Marjorie Campoli

Oral Warning to Marjorie Campoli
From: Joanne Papacostos
RE: Personal Telephone Calls

I spoke to Marjorie Campoli today regarding her violating our customer service pclicy to keep all telephone lines open for customers exclusively. I heard Marjorie making plans for a party when she was at her work station at 3:00 p.m. I reviewed the policy regarding personal calls. She understands that she is to make personal calls during lunch or her breaks and to use the public telephone provided. She has agreed to comply with all policies regarding telephone calls.

Use the following form to write a warning for Marjorie based on her conversation and the file document. Incorporate all eight documentation rules into your warning.

WARNING NOTICE

Employee: _____ Date: _____

On the above date, I warned the above-named employee concerning the following:

_____
_____
_____
_____
_____
_____
_____
_____

This warning places the employee in probationary status for a period of _____ days. The employee may not be considered for a salary increase nor permitted to apply for another job opening. If the above incident reoccurs during the next _____ days the result will be:

____ Second written warning

____ Suspension

____ Discharge for misconduct

_____   _____
Supervisor's Signature   Date

I acknowledge that I have received a copy of the above warning.

_____   _____
Employee's Signature   Date

■ Written Warning Scorecard

Use the following scorecard to evaluate your written warning for Marjorie. Circle Y (yes) or N (no).

Y N   **1.** Did I state that the reason for taking disciplinary action was continued policy violation?

Y N   **2.** Did I state that this was a formal written warning?

Y N   **3.** Did I describe the overheard personal conversation?

Y N   **4.** Did I refer to the oral warning and Marjorie's earlier commitment?

Y N   **5.** Did I cite the facts? (Marjorie placed her personal call on hold to answer customer calls.)

Y N   **6.** Did I use easy-to-understand language?

Y N   **7.** Did I avoid subjective statements and potentially discriminatory language and phrases?

Y N   **8.** Did I avoid exaggeration in my description of Marjorie's use of the telephone? (Focused on use of the telephone rather than on "excessive number of personal calls.")

Y N   **9.** Did I indicate what the consequences were if Marjorie did not comply with the policy on personal telephone calls?

If you have circled all *Y*s, then you have successfully included all the eight documentation points in your written warning for Marjorie. If you have circled any *N*s, reread the managers' discussion at the beginning of the chapter to clarify any points you missed.

You can see from this chapter how important documentation is to the disciplinary process. Without it, it is difficult to take action to correct employee problems. You can also see that documentation can be straightforward and easy to do, once you've practiced the eight steps shown.

Chapter 5 Checkpoints

Does Your Document—

✓ Clearly state the reason for the warning?

✓ Indicate that it is an oral warning, a written warning (first, second, etc.), or suspension?

✓ Identify the specific violation or offense that prompted the warning?

✓ Describe the incident? Include the date, time, employees involved, location, sequence of events?

✓ Put facts in a logical order that is readily understood by the reader?

✓ Avoid any derogatory comments about the employee or the employee's habits, morals, or person?

✓ Avoid language that could be discriminatory? (References to an employee's age, color, sex, race, national origin, disabilities, or Vietnam-era veteran status.)

✓ Avoid exaggerating the event and the reactions of others?

✓ Clearly tell the employee what the consequences of continued behavior means?

6 | Getting Commitment

This chapter will help you to:

- Obtain commitment for real change.
- Identify actions that both you and your employee can take for successful behavior change.
- Be clear about the outcome you desire.
- Develop follow-up plans.
- Support the outcomes you and your employee have created.

YOUR OBJECTIVES

A disciplinary discussion has three main objectives:

1. To tell the employee what he or she has done and why it requires formal disciplinary action.
2. To explain consequences to the employee if no change occurs within a specific time frame.
3. To obtain commitment for change.

A discussion that meets these three objectives usually resolves the problem.

Disciplinary discussions should *not* be used to:

Punish or humiliate employees.

Vent anger or hostility.

"Get even" for past mistakes.

Show employees who's boss.

Threaten or coerce employees.

Discussions that dissolve into "venting" sessions rarely obtain any needed change and usually create more problems.

THE MANAGER'S ROLE

To ensure an effective outcome, there are three steps all effective managers should take in the disciplinary discussion.

1. Explain the Problem.   Effective managers begin their disciplinary discussions by clearly explaining the problem and the impact of the problem.

> "Mason, for the last two weeks you have been taking three times as long to count your cash drawer because you have been on the telephone with personal calls. This creates a real problem because all the other cashiers have to wait until you finish."

2. Obtain Commitment.   Effective managers listen to their employees, assist them with ideas for solving the problem, and obtain real commitment.

> "Let's review what you have agreed to do: You've agreed to make a brief call to check on your children before you start cash count. Then you'll resume your standard balancing time so that we can all get out on time."

3. Monitor Progress.   Effective managers actively monitor employee progress and follow up by speaking to the employee about what they see.

> "Thanks, Mason, I see we are all getting out on time. How are your children doing after school now?"

■ **T h i n k   a b o u t   I t**

Which of the three steps do you carry out most effectively?

_____

Which of the three steps do you carry out least effectively?

_____

What do you need to do to improve your disciplinary discussions?

_____

Car Trouble

Nick Gigliotti is somewhat satisfied as he leaves the conference room where he has spent a half hour with his newest computer operator trainee, Brian Mullaney. Brian, a newlywed, had left before completing the special computer test runs because his wife needed the car to get to her night job. Nick had spoken to Brian before about leaving without finishing work. In this session, Nick gave Brian an oral warning. Now Nick refers to his notes. Brian has agreed to:

1. Resolve transportation problem with wife.

2. Complete jobs even if they require staying beyond normal scheduled hours.

3. Ask one of the senior operators for assistance.

Nick is still not sure if Brian understands that this job requires flexibility in staying late on occasion or coming in at night when there is a problem. Nick regrets saying that Brian should have shown common sense and asked for help. All the other operators have been there so long that they automatically know what to do or whom to ask for help. He should not have expected Brian to have that level of experience. Nick decides to list some things that he will do to follow up with Brian.

If you were Nick what would you include in your list of follow-up activities?

_____

_____

_____

_____

> **Tip** ─────────────────────────────
>
> Use your policy manual, job description, and other written materials to reinforce both employer expectations and the importance of the employee meeting these expectations.

THE EMPLOYEE'S ROLE

After an open, honest discussion, the employee should understand his or her role, and should follow these corrective actions:

1. Recognize the Problem.   Employees who want to make their best contributions to your organization will want to correct problems in order to succeed in the company.

> "John, I'm sorry. I didn't realize I was creating a problem for everyone else. I don't blame them for wanting to get home on time. I was just so concerned because this is the first year my kids have no one with them after school."

2. Accept Responsibility.   Employees who take responsibility for their actions usually have workable solutions to the problems or are willing to take others' suggestions for solving the problems seriously.

> "I'll talk with my kids tonight so they will understand what is going on. We will have to talk about their day when I get home. And keep our phone call as a check in call. But I do need to make that call once a day."

3. Commit to Change. Employees who commit to change and succeed feel better about themselves, and often continue to be productive contributors in the workplace.

> "Thanks for asking about the kids. They're fine. You know, what we do now is turn off the TV when I come home. I sit down and listen and they show me all their school things. It seems to be working out."

▮ Think about It

What correction actions do your employees seem to find easiest to do? Why?

_____

_____

_____

In your experience, what correction actions are most difficult for employees? Why?

_____

_____

Brian's Dilemma

Brian is uncomfortable the day after his discussion with Nick. Brian's wife was angry and indignant that he received a reprimand because she needed the car to go to work. Brian did not explain to her that he could lose his job if he didn't work the required hours. He knows that he will have a problem keeping his commitment to Nick. Brian decides to make an appointment with the personnel director to discuss his dilemma.

What advice would you give Brian to resolve his dilemma?

_____

_____

_____

6

How do you handle an employee's inability to keep a commitment due to an outside conflict?

_____
_____
_____
_____

What are some creative solutions to Brian's problem?

_____
_____
_____
_____

6

> **Tip**
>
> Recognize that outside commitments and conflicts can hamper an employee's ability to come up with workable solutions. Employees need your ideas and support to balance their commitments.

Car Compromise

It has been thirty days since Nick agreed not to assign end-of-day special runs to Brian. And, today, Brian is the owner of a secondhand car that he will use to drive to work while his wife uses their new car. Brian knows now that he will have no difficulty keeping his time commitments to his job. Although Brian was reluctant to compromise at first, Nick can now see the difference in his behavior. ■

SHARPEN YOUR PROBLEM-SOLVING SKILLS

After each scenario, identify the specific problem that needs correction and develop three ways for the employee to resolve the problem.

Case One

You are the proprietor of an upscale family restaurant in an area where five other restaurants compete for business. For some reason, Eduardo, a very bright graduate student, still is not greeting your customers properly when he takes their orders. You observe that he does not smile, mumbles when he gets to the table, and looks out the window when the customers are looking over the selections. At the last table, he did not give the customers the specials for the day. In spite of the fact that Eduardo will come in whenever you are short-staffed, his continued lack of customer courtesy is becoming a serious problem. ■

The problem is: _____

_____

List three employee actions that would resolve the problem:

6

1. _____

2. _____

3. _____

Case Two

In your company, three supervisors report to you. You are concerned about the leadership skills of Annette, who supervises 25 clerks in an open office format. You noted some specific problems on her last review, but she has not taken them seriously. Annette continues to have piles of folders on her desk and on the floor by her chair, and cups of unfinished coffee dotting the piles of folders and windowsill. When she wants to speak to one of her clerks, she shouts across the room and many of the clerks stop what they are doing to see what is going on. Her two peers avoid her because she is disruptive and talks too much. ■

The problem is: _____
_____

List three ways Annette can resolve the problem:

1. _____

2. _____

3. _____

Case Three

You have traced the source of the late reports to the senior production clerk, who is supposed to supply daily production figures to your department. From what you gather, she is a smoker and sneaks two to five smoke breaks a day. Before the smoke-free building policy was in effect, her smoking was not a problem because the lounge was across from her office. Now, she must leave the building to smoke. This takes too much time, and as a result her daily reports are late. ■

The problem is: _____
_____

List three employee actions to resolve the problem:

1. _____

2. _____

3. _____

EXPLAINING THE CONSEQUENCES

Before discussion with an employee about a problem, consider the consequences and be prepared to communicate what will happen should the employee not change behavior and conform to policy.

The chart shown here provides a guide to consequences based on the use of a progressive disciplinary process. This list is not all-inclusive. The circumstances of each case and company policy may offer other alternatives or consequences.

Progressive Action	Consequences for No Change
Oral warning	Written warning
Written warning	Second written warning if: Minor infraction Difficult behavior change Extenuating circumstances
	Suspension or termination if: Major policy violation Threat to others Deliberate insubordination
Suspension	Additional suspension if: Minor infraction Difficult behavior change
	Termination if: Major policy violation Threat to others Deliberate insubordination

Employees need to understand what will occur if they do not change their behavior or comply with the company policies. Most disciplinary discussions end with a summary of consequences and a reiteration of the importance of change.

FOLLOW UP WITH ONGOING SUPPORT

Effective managers agree to solutions for change, and ensure employee success by monitoring their employees' progress and by offering encouragement and direction. The purpose of follow-up is to ensure permanent change.

The employee action or inaction is identified in the following list. Supply what you think the appropriate management support follow-up should be in the corresponding column. The first example is completed for you.

6

Employee Action	Management Support
Arrives on time each day for first week of agreement.	Congratulates the employee publicly for coming in on time.
Produces an accurately measured cut-and-paste layout on own after retraining period.	
Fails to ask for help from others and is late with report again. Is not keeping to agreement.	
Still has difficulty answering the telephone but has mastered the greeting and opening lines well.	
Has not made one personal long distance telephone call during the probation period.	
After one week of exemplary behavior, is now back to wandering through departments during the day.	
Is now on time for every meeting but has stopped making any idea contributions to the task force.	
Again, left work in the middle of the shift without telling supervisor.	

Chapter 6 Checkpoints

✓ Can I explain what the problem is and why it is a problem in terms my employee can grasp?

✓ Am I committed to the consequences if my employee does not change?

✓ Do I have some alternative solutions in case my employee has no ideas?

✓ Is my documentation complete?

✓ Do I have a general follow-up plan in mind? Am I prepared to handle non-job-related reasons for the problem?

✓ Have I consulted my policy handbook?

✓ Am I up to date with my company practices and procedures for handling similar cases?

7 | Common Employee Problems

This chapter will help you to:

- Evaluate typical employee problems.
- Determine the most appropriate corrective or disciplinary action to take in each situation.

PUTTING YOUR SKILLS TO WORK

This chapter places you in three different managerial situations. Your mission in each case is to:

- Determine the nature of the problem.
- Assess the seriousness of the situation.
- Make some assumptions about the employee based on the case description and the documents.
- Determine what type of corrective action is called for.
- Complete the appropriate documentation.
- Describe the steps you will take.

As you read each situation, put yourself in the manager's shoes and complete the Situation Evaluation form at the end of the case study. If you decide the situation needs documentation, prepare a warning notice using the blank Warning Notice form. When you've evaluated each case, answer the questions at the end of the case study.

The Situation Evaluation form following each case provides a shorthand method of rating the situation and assists in selecting corrective action based on your completed evaluation. The following sample Situation Evaluation has been completed using the example of Louis Garcia from Chapter 4.

SITUATION EVALUATION

Employee: __Louis Garcia_____ Job Title: __Shipper_____
Problem: __Frequent tardiness_____
Last Discussion: __Last Wednesday_____

Seriousness of problem:

|_____|_____X_____|_____|
Minor   Mid   Major

Impact on other workers:

|_____|_____X__|_____|
Minor   Mid   Major

Employee overall performance rating:

|_____|____X____|_____|
Unsatisfactory   Satisfactory   Outstanding

Employee attitude:

|_____|X_____|_____|
Closed   Neutral   Open

ACTION TO TAKE

Select One	Check Situation Match
Corrective discussion	___ First discussion. No serious violation.
Oral warning	XX No change after correction.
	___ Minor infraction of policy.
	___ Minor loss/injury involved.
Written warning	___ Did not respond to oral warning with immediate changes.
	___ Major infraction of policy.
	___ Serious loss/injury involved.
Suspension	___ Is violent. Danger to self and others.
	___ Serious infraction requires investigation.
	___ Fails to heed written warnings.

The Case of Ed Evergone

You filled a job opening in your department four months ago with an internal candidate, Ed Evergone. As you look at Ed's attendance cards, you wonder if, indeed, someone neglected to give you all the details on Ed. His performance evaluations make no mention of attendance problems. He is rated highly competent in his last appraisal.

In the four months Ed has been in your department, Ed has been absent eight days—one day here, two days there. And Ed is usually out at the busiest periods of the month or on Fridays. You are not convinced that Ed has been ill on any of these occasions.

His absence this morning is especially provoking because it is the end of the month, and another member of your staff is on vacation. You decide to review his previous attendance record and notice a similar pattern. Interestingly enough, Ed never exceeded his allotted paid sick time.

Ed's absences are also causing some friction among members of your staff. You overheard two of them grumbling about *always* having to take care of Evergone's work. *What action will you take?* ■

7

Ed's Attendance Record						
Week	Mon	Tues	Wed	Thurs	Fri	Sat/Sun
1						
2	Sick					
3						
4			Sick			
5						
6	Sick	Sick				
7						
8						
9			Sick		Sick	
10						
11						
12					Sick	
13						
14					Sick	
15						
16			Today!!			

SITUATION EVALUATION

Employee: _____ Job Title: _____

Problem: _____

Last Discussion: _____

Seriousness of problem:

                Minor   **Mid**   **Major**

Impact on other workers:

                Minor   **Mid**   **Major**

Employee overall performance rating:

    Unsatisfactory   **Satisfactory**   **Outstanding**

Employee attitude:

                Closed   **Neutral**   **Open**

ACTION TO TAKE

Select One	**Check Situation Match**
Corrective discussion	___ First discussion. No serious violation.
Oral warning	___ No change after correction.
	___ Minor infraction of policy.
	___ Minor loss/injury involved.
Written warning	___ Did not respond to oral warning with immediate changes.
	___ Major infraction of policy.
	___ Serious loss/injury involved.
Suspension	___ Is violent. Danger to self and others.
	___ Serious infraction requires investigation.
	___ Fails to heed written warnings.

WARNING NOTICE

Employee: _____ Date: _____

_____

_____

_____

_____

_____

_____

If the above incident reoccurs during the next _____ days the result will be:

___ Second written warning   ___ Suspension

___ Discharge for misconduct

_____   _____

Supervisor's Signature   Date

Questions to Consider

7

1. In your company, what is considered abusive use of sick days?

_____

_____

_____

2. In this case study did the manager wait too long? Why or why not?

_____

_____

_____

3. In your opinion can chronic sick-day abusers be cured?

_____

_____

_____

The Case of Peter Perfect

Peter Perfect is the most competent programmer in your section. He is well organized, a master at planning, and never misses a detail. Because of his abilities, Peter receives the most complex assignments. Without fail, he completes each program well ahead of schedule.

Peter Perfect is also probably the most obnoxious "so and so" east of the Mississippi. In his desire to execute perfect programs, he treats users with contempt, snaps at his coworkers, and refuses interruptions. Although you have counseled Peter and suggested ways to improve his working relationships (which, you emphasized, were vital to his advancement—his most sensitive interest), little has changed.

You have just had a very emotional meeting with Craig Cusson, the vice president of another section, regarding Peter Perfect's abusive behavior. Peter spoke so sharply to one of Craig's supervisors that she was in tears and did not want to work with Peter again. Craig wants you to reassign the project to someone else. But you have no one else who is competent enough to complete the project. *What action will you take?* ■

7

SITUATION EVALUATION

Employee: _____ Job Title: _____

Problem: _____

Last Discussion: _____

Seriousness of problem:

Minor   Mid   Major

Impact on other workers:

Minor   Mid   Major

Employee overall performance rating:

Unsatisfactory   Satisfactory   Outstanding

Employee attitude:

Closed   Neutral   Open

ACTION TO TAKE

7

Select One	Check Situation Match
Corrective discussion	___ First discussion. No serious violation.
Oral warning	___ No change after correction.
	___ Minor infraction of policy.
	___ Minor loss/injury involved.
Written warning	___ Did not respond to oral warning with immediate changes.
	___ Major infraction of policy.
	___ Serious loss/injury involved.
Suspension	___ Is violent. Danger to self and others.
	___ Serious infraction requires investigation.
	___ Fails to heed written warnings.

WARNING NOTICE

Employee: _____ Date: _____

_____

_____

_____

_____

_____

_____

_____

If the above incident reoccurs during the next _____ days the result will be:

___ Second written warning   ___   Suspension

___ Discharge for misconduct

_____   _____
Supervisor's Signature   Date

7

Questions to Consider

1. What are the major difficulties you face in motivating highly technical people to improve their interaction skills?

_____

_____

_____

2. What do you think is the most effective way to assist people in improving their interpersonal skills?

_____

_____

_____

3. In this case, what will you use as motivation for Peter Perfect?

_____

_____

_____

The Case of Wilma Wontdo

You are the new manager of an operations department. You have been on this job for three months. You are responsible for automating many of the manual functions performed by this department. You have a 25-person staff, many of whom are long-term employees.

Wilma Wontdo is one of these employees. You have just finished a blistering conversation with an irate customer service manager regarding Wilma's rudeness and ineptitude. Wilma refused to give information to a customer and brusquely told the customer it wasn't her job. The customer called the customer service manager, who relayed the problem to you.

This is not the first such complaint. In fact, it was the third complaint this week. Two weeks ago you had reviewed Wilma and discussed other complaints on her lack of cooperation. Moreover, you pointed out that she was making far too many spelling errors on customer accounts. Wilma had reacted very defensively to your comments. She refused to acknowledge any errors. She said that no one complained about her before and that she had been in the department for 10 years and certainly knew all the functions. She said she was having no problems with using the new computer system.

In your opinion, Wilma resents you as the new supervisor and resents any and all changes to "her" department. As far as you can determine, Wilma lacks basic skills such as spelling, reading, and doing simple math calculations needed for completing her job functions. You are wondering how Wilma has managed to hang on to her job for so long. Before you sit down with Wilma you decide to read her file, which you had not read prior to taking over the department. ■

7

PERFORMANCE REPORT

Name: Wilma Wontdo   Reason: Annual   Date: 3/93
Title: Customer Records Clerk   Dept: 45   Pay Grade: 6

Instructions: Supervisors use numeric ratings listed below.
Ratings: 1 = Unsatisfactory; 2 = Does not fully meet standards; 3 = Fully meets standards; 4 = Exceeds standards

Performance Criteria:	Supervisor's Ratings			
	1	2	3	4
Quality of work Consider accuracy and thoroughness in completing assignments.			X	
Quantity of work Consider volume produced or number of assignments completed.				X
Dependability Consider reliability and promptness in completing assignments, amount of supervision required.				X
Efficiency Consider organization of work, ability to meet deadlines.				X
Attitude Consider interest in work, attitude toward department, others, customers.				X

Performance summary and rating:
Clearly exceeds most job standards.

Supervisor's comments:
Wilma is very cooperative and willing to learn. She has cross-trained in two additional functions. She makes very few errors. Those she makes she corrects without supervisory help. I feel she is ready to move to a higher position.

Employee's comments:
I feel I have done a good job in learning all the new jobs in our department. I am interested in advancement with the company.

PERFORMANCE REPORT

Name: Wilma Wontdo   Reason: Annual   Date: 3/92

Title: Customer Records Clerk   Dept: 45   Pay Grade: 6

Instructions: Supervisors use numeric ratings listed below.
Ratings: 1 = Unsatisfactory; 2 = Does not fully meet standards; 3 = Fully meets standards; 4 = Exceeds standards

Performance Criteria:	Supervisor's Ratings			
	1	2	3	4
Quality of work Consider accuracy and thoroughness in completing assignments.			X	
Quantity of work Consider volume produced or number of assignments completed.			X	
Dependability Consider reliability and promptness in completing assignments, amount of supervision required.			X	
Efficiency Consider organization of work, ability to meet deadlines.			X	
Attitude Consider interest in work, attitude toward department, others, customers.			X	

Performance summary and rating:
Performance fully meets all job standards.

Supervisor's comments:
Wilma has exceptional knowledge of her job. Needs to be open to learning some new tasks. She has had a few problems with her coworkers but her attitude is improving.

Employee's comments:
I feel I have done a good job and am anxious to learn more.

Now that you have read Wilma's Performance Reports for the past two years, *what action will you take?*

SITUATION EVALUATION

Employee: _____   Job Title: _____

Problem: _____

Last Discussion: _____

Seriousness of problem:

      Minor   Mid   Major

Impact on other workers:

      Minor   Mid   Major

Employee overall performance rating:

      Unsatisfactory   Competent   Outstanding

Employee attitude:

      Closed   Neutral   Open

7

ACTION TO TAKE

Select One	Check Situation Match
Corrective discussion	___ First discussion. No serious violation.
Oral warning	___ No change after correction.
	___ Minor infraction of policy.
	___ Minor loss/injury involved.
Written warning	___ Did not respond to oral warning with immediate changes.
	___ Major infraction of policy.
	___ Serious loss/injury involved.
Suspension	___ Is violent. Danger to self and others.
	___ Serious infraction requires investigation.
	___ Fails to heed written warnings.

WARNING NOTICE

Employee: _____ Date: _____

_____

_____

_____

_____

_____

_____

_____

If the above incident reoccurs during the next _____ days the result will be:

___ Second written warning   ___ Suspension

___ Discharge for misconduct

_____   _____

Supervisor's Signature   Date

Questions to Consider

1. This case study presents several problems. What problem will you tackle first?

_____

_____

_____

2. What do you do when an employee's past performance appraisals do not match current performance expectations? Are there special difficulties when this happens with a long-term employee?

_____

_____

_____

3. Develop a long-term action plan for dealing with Wilma.

_____

_____

_____

Chapter 7 Checkpoints

✓ Carefully examine all aspects of a case before taking action.

✓ Take action that is in line with your company policies and practices.

✓ Consider the employee's behavior patterns and the difficulty of changing them when constructing a time frame for improvement.

✓ Select consequences that are appropriate to the infraction or violation.

8 The Disciplinary Interview and Follow-Up

This chapter will help you to:

- Conduct the disciplinary interview.
- State the consequences and prepare to follow up.
- Recognize the need for active employee involvement and commitment to lasting solutions.
- Be consistent in the disciplinary process.
- Gain *positive* results.

THE DISCIPLINARY INTERVIEW: KEYS TO SUCCESS

While the disciplinary interview is similar to the correctional discussion, its tone is more formal and serious. Preparing formal documentation and treating the action as part of a progressive process changes the finale of the discussion.

Five Steps to Follow for the Interview

1. Describe the problem and the seriousness of the problem. Refer to prior discussions or to company policy.
2. Confirm the details of the most recent incident with the employee.
3. Discover the reasons for employee behavior or noncompliance with past agreements.
4. Agree on or reaffirm solutions to the problem.
5. Describe the disciplinary action you are taking and why. Summarize the plan of action and the consequences.

> ## ▮ Tip
>
> Stay focused on the problem you are trying to resolve. Do not be sidetracked by excuses or attempts at blaming others. The more problem-focused you are, the more likely you will be able to control the emotional climate of the interview.

Make a Lasting Commitment

As you work through the disciplinary process with an employee, you may be concerned about ensuring consistent and fair treatment to all employees. As a manager, you have a responsibility to maintain lasting standards of performance and discipline for all employees, including yourself. To make the correction process work over time, you need to first define your role, and then get active employee involvement in the process.

In the following case, we find ourselves with Wilma and her supervisor from Chapter 7. As you read the case, consider the effectiveness of the five-step plan for disciplinary interviews.

In the memo that follows, Jolene provides written documentation of the disciplinary interview. The memo clearly states the outcome of the interview and lays out a plan of action and its consequences.

Jolene:

Wilma, please sit down. We need to talk about . . .

Wilma:

I hope you are not going to complain about me again.

Jolene:

Wilma, please. I need to speak to you specifically about handling customer telephone calls into the department.

Wilma:

You spoke to me about that last week. Really, Jolene, I'm not stupid. I can handle the customers on the telephone.

Jolene:

I would like you to hear me out. Yesterday afternoon you received a call from Dolores Rivera. She had a problem with her account. You told her you could not help her—that, and I quote, "the girl who does that is not here, you can call back tomorrow." Mrs. Rivera was very upset and called Marcy, the customer service manager. Marcy placated Mrs. Rivera and solved her problem. Is this what happened?

Wilma:

Well, it was Mary Lou she needed to speak to. I couldn't help her. It wasn't my fault.

Jolene:

Last week I spoke to you about how to handle a customer call. I gave you specific steps to follow. We wrote those down. Why didn't you use them?

Wilma:

I didn't remember the steps. You know, it's very confusing. I don't know how you expect me to think of everything when I'm answering the phone. Besides, she had an accent and I could hardly understand her.

Jolene:

Wilma, do you remember the specific steps I told you?

Wilma:

Of course I do. It's easy to remember them when I'm not on the phone.

Jolene:

What did you fail to do for Mrs. Rivera?

Wilma:

I don't know. I just couldn't help her.

Jolene:

Specifically, you forgot to get all the facts. If you find you cannot solve the customer problem immediately, take the customer's name and number and call him or her back when you have the problem solved.

Wilma:

Well, I was busy. I was the only one there. I don't think you should pick on me for one mistake.

Jolene:

Two of the last three times we have spoken about customer responses have revolved around your not getting the facts. Now Wilma, what are you going to do about this?

Wilma:

I don't know. I keep forgetting.

Jolene:

Let me suggest that you tape a copy of the procedure right above your phone. Underline "get the facts" so you see it clearly. Do you think that will help?

Wilma:

I suppose it might.

Jolene:

What else might help?

Wilma:

I guess that should do it. We have talked about it enough.

Jolene:

Now Wilma, I want to make it very clear to you that answering our customer telephone calls is a priority part of the job. It's as important as inputting customer information into the computer.

Wilma:

I can't see it. I've been here 10 years and getting the data in has always been the most important thing. We never had to answer customer calls.

Jolene:

The way we do business has changed. Correcting or changing customer information through a quick customer call is now part of how we've become more efficient and sensitive to our customers' needs. Wilma, will you agree to handle the customer calls according to our standards?

Wilma:

I'll try. But I'm not perfect, you know.

Jolene:

Wilma, it has to be *do*, not *try*. (Pauses.) Because I sense real reluctance on your part to change, and because we've had three conversations on the topic of handling customer telephone calls, I've prepared an oral warning for your file.

Wilma:

What?!!

8

Jolene:

I'm sorry, Wilma. I know that you've always had a good record in the past. How-ever, for whatever reason, you aren't making any effort to handle customers over the telephone to meet our customer service standards.

Wilma:

I don't think that's fair at all.

Jolene:

I don't know how else to convince you that this change in the way we do business is real and permanent. You must handle customers differently. This is a company mandate.

Here is a copy of the warning. The purpose is to alert you to the seriousness of the situation. I fully expect that you'll be able to make this change.

You've been in the department for ten years. And you've been through many changes. I know you've been very instrumental in making some of those changes. You can do this. But it's up to you.

Wilma:

Can I think about this? Can we talk again?

Jolene:

Yes, of course, think about this. And I'll be happy to speak to you again. Here, take the copy with you. Please notice that if you don't take this warning seriously you could receive a written warning.

Wilma:

Oh? All right. I'll talk to you later.

Jolene:

Okay. Let me know. ■

WILMA'S WARNING MEMO

To: Wilma Wontdo
From: Jolene Stillwell
Date: October 14, 1993

Oral Warning

Today, I spoke to Wilma regarding the proper response to customer calls into the department. This was the fourth discussion in the last three weeks that we have had on this topic.

Specifically, the incident which prompted this warning was Wilma's failure to assist Dolores Rivera, a customer who called in with a mailing address correction. Wilma refused to help and told Mrs. Rivera to call back tomorrow. Mrs. Rivera called the customer service manager who relayed the incident to me.

I have suggested that Wilma paste up a copy of the company procedure for handling customer calls over her telephone, and highlight the instructions on how to help a customer.

I expect that Wilma will follow the company procedure for handling all incoming customer calls and that I will receive no more customer complaints.

If Wilma fails to take this oral warning seriously and does not meet our service standards, she may be subject to a written warning as the next step.

Questions to Consider

8

1. How well did Jolene stay focused on the problem during the interview with Wilma?

_____

_____

_____

2. What was Wilma's main reason for not complying with the change?

_____

_____

_____

3. What impact does an oral warning have on an employee like Wilma? Will she change?

_____

_____

_____

4. What successes have you had in changing employee behavior after they understood the importance of making some changes?

_____

_____

_____

HANDLING EMPLOYEE REACTIONS

When an employee understands that formal action will be taken, he or she may become emotional. Some employees may feel

Threatened with impending job loss.

Immediate loss of self-esteem.

Anger and need to lash out.

Depressed and despondent.

These are usually temporary emotional states. Your goal is to move the employee beyond destructive emotions and prompt a desire by the employee to achieve the agreed-on actions.

Be Supportive

While you should be sensitive to your employee's reactions, you want to focus your actions on positive support for an employee change in behavior or return to upholding company policies. Management support includes the following:

1. **Acknowledging employee's negative feelings and redirecting the employee's focus.**

   "I know you are still upset with me about the warning. I'd like to see you move beyond your anger and get moving on completing this project. It's a showcase project for you."

2. **Acknowledging and recognizing employee improvement.**

   "Wilma, I heard you on the phone just now with that customer. Your response was perfect—your tone so friendly and helpful. Great! Keep it up."

3. **Acknowledging that mistakes will occur and encouraging employee to self-correct.**

   "Wilson, I know we said no more imperfect sheets and this one has a flaw. You know how to fix it. Now go on and do it."

4. **Acknowledging the employee's effort to improve and supporting the employee to the next step.**

   "Not bad, Marie. You are definitely prepared to give the presentation. Tonight, go home and practice in front of the mirror. Then you'll be fine."

5. **Acknowledging the employee's compliance with rules and citing positive impact.**

   "Thanks for being on time. We haven't missed a shipment deadline all week."

8

WHERE DO YOU FIT IN?

At this point, let's briefly recap your role in the process. Why are you expected to discipline? What's in it for you, and for your company?

Your Role as Manager

Your key function as a manager is to ensure that your department completes its work on time in the most effective manner and with an eye to maintaining required standards for cost and performance. How your department operates and how your employees perform is a direct reflection of how well you direct and lead them.

The results of effectively supervising difficult employees and strained situations are that you will:

- Command the attention and respect of your employees.
- Prevent work issues from building up and creating decline in levels of service and performance.
- Keep your employees focused on actual work outcomes.
- Reduce work stress for yourself and your employees.
- Maintain a healthy *esprit de corps* for all team members.

Your Voice as Manager

8

As a member of the management team, you represent the company through your actions and words. You are the company's clearest example of what the company stands for. You are charged with upholding company policy and with enforcing company rules.

The results of representing the company consistently when you are faced with policy violations are that your employees will:

- Understand company policy and practices.
- Strive to follow company rules and regulations.
- Know that there are no favorites and that all will be treated according to company standards.
- Set examples for new employees to follow.
- Demonstrate loyalty to fair leadership.

Your Task as Coach

To meet the increasing demands for productivity and service, you are expected to direct and coach your employees to their highest levels of performance achievement. You identify, assign, and motivate your employees to succeed as individuals and as members of teams.

The benefits of reducing employee tension levels through sensitive handling of difficult or contentious employees are that you will:

- Stop individual behavior that adversely impacts your team.
- Give the offending employee the opportunity to begin anew and reestablish his/her level of acceptable performance.
- Revitalize the team with renewed commitment to team goals.
- Affirm positive behavior as the means to success.
- Reduce negative talk among members of the team.

CONSISTENCY COUNTS

8

The value of a consistent, progressive disciplinary process is that you and your employees know what to expect. If employees abuse sick time, they receive a deserved oral warning. If employees commit a serious infraction, such as defacing company property, they know that they face a written warning and possibly a suspension. The rules apply to all employees.

Progressive disciplinary procedures give the employee an opportunity to change behavior and to get back on track with the other members of the team. Clear directives and realistic timetables can help ensure success for the employee.

Finally, effective discipline sends clear messages to all of your employees: certain behavior is not acceptable, company safety rules are serious, courteous interaction is expected at all times, and so forth. Order restored to the worksite means that all employees can get back to the business of working.

Employee Involvement

Your timely action in supervising difficult employees is often the trigger for obtaining an employee's commitment to solving the situation. If you act promptly and do not allow an employee to develop poor work habits or continue to violate company policy, you will most likely be able to resolve the problem quickly.

The longer an employee is allowed to act or perform below acceptable standards, the more difficult it is for the employee to accept the need for change. Yet, it is the employee who must change. Your task is to ensure that employees understand the consequences of their actions and the necessity for immediate changes. With an employee's complete understanding comes commitment, and from commitment comes change.

Process Failure

In some cases, the disciplinary process fails. The employee does not change behavior—the employee continues to violate policies or is unable to provide consistent changes. Where the disciplinary process fails, your alternatives are to change the job or change the employee.

Occasionally, an employee's behavior is caused by an inability to perform the current job, or by an inappropriate job assignment. You may choose to place the employee in a job better suited to his or her talents and skills.

In most cases where the disciplinary process fails the employee is terminated. Timely, complete documentation will support and justify the need for termination. The end should not come as a surprise to the employee who is fully apprised of consequences throughout the various stages of the disciplinary process.

Disciplinary documents are part of the employee's personnel file. Accurate and complete documentation is necessary to defend you and your company against unnecessary unemployment compensation claims, illegal termination charges, and other individual grievances that can follow an employee's termination.

Tips

Rules to Remember

Command employee respect by confronting difficult employees and redirecting their efforts.

Let your actions demonstrate company values. Expect your employees to follow your example.

Give your employees the opportunity to improve and grow in their daily tasks.

Protect yourself and your company by following a consistent, thoughtful disciplinary process.

Demonstrate your support for changes and expect your employees to succeed.

8

Chapter 8 Checkpoints

✓ Stay focused on resolving the problem to help control the emotional climate.

✓ Complete the interview with the formal action.

✓ Make sure the employee understands the consequences of non-compliance with the agreements.

✓ Support the positive actions of your employee to bring about quicker resolution.

✓ Always be consistent in the disciplinary process.

✓ Employee commitment is the best measure of willingness to change—aim for commitment!

Post-Test

Complete each statement below.

1. Blatant or deliberate violation of company policies requires a manager to _____.

2. Employees continue disruptive behavior if they _____ _____.

3. Progressive disciplinary actions include _____ _____.

4. _____ is usually the first step in dealing with employees who create problems.

5. The five steps to conducting a corrective discussion are: _____ _____.

6. Company practices offer pointers on how to handle _____ _____.

7. Terminating an employee results when the _____ _____.

8. _____ can help prevent future discrimination charges.

9. The impact of disciplinary action on an employee may include _____ _____.

10. Two examples of management support actions are: _____ _____.

Business Skills Express Series

This growing series of books addresses a broad range of key business skills and topics to meet the needs of employees, human resource departments, and training consultants.

To obtain information about these and other Business Skills Express books, please call Irwin Professional Publishing toll free at: 1-800-634-3966.

Effective Performance Management
ISBN   1-55623-867-3

Hiring the Best
ISBN   1-55623-865-7

Writing that Works
ISBN   1-55623-856-8

Customer Service Excellence
ISBN   1-55623-969-6

Writing for Business Results
ISBN   1-55623-854-1

Powerful Presentation Skills
ISBN   1-55623-870-3

Meetings that Work
ISBN   1-55623-866-5

Effective Teamwork
ISBN   1-55623-880-0

Time Management
ISBN   1-55623-888-6

Assertiveness Skills
ISBN   1-55623-857-6

Motivation at Work
ISBN   1-55623-868-1

Overcoming Anxiety at Work
ISBN   1-55623-869-X

Positive Politics at Work
ISBN   1-55623-879-7

Telephone Skills at Work
ISBN   1-55623-858-4

Managing Conflict at Work
ISBN   1-55623-890-8

The New Supervisor: Skills for Success
ISBN   1-55623-762-6

The *Americans with Disabilities Act:* What Supervisors Need to Know
ISBN   1-55623-889-4

Managing the Demands of Work and Home
ISBN   0-7863-0221-6

Effective Listening Skills
ISBN   0-7863-0102-4

Goal Management at Work
ISBN   0-7863-0225-9

Positive Attitudes at Work
ISBN   0-7863-0100-8

Supervising the Difficult Employee
ISBN   0-7863-0219-4

Cultural Diversity in the Workplace
ISBN   0-7863-0125-2

Managing Change in the Workplace
ISBN   0-7863-0162-7

Negotiating for Business Results
ISBN   0-7863-0114-7

Practical Business Communication
ISBN   0-7863-0227-5

High Performance Speaking
ISBN   0-7863-0222-4

Delegation Skills
ISBN   0-7863-0105-9

Coaching Skills: A Guide for Supervisors
ISBN   0-7863-0220-8

Customer Service and the Telephone
ISBN   0-7863-0224-0

Creativity at Work
ISBN   0-7863-0223-2

Effective Interpersonal Relationships
ISBN   0-7863-0255-0

The Participative Leader
ISBN   0-7863-0252-6

Building Customer Loyalty
ISBN   0-7863-0253-4

Getting and Staying Organized
ISBN   0-7863-0254-2

Total Quality Selling
ISBN   0-7863-0324-7

Business Etiquette
ISBN   0-7863-0323-9

Empowering Employees
ISBN   0-7863-0314-X

Training Skills for Supervisors
ISBN   0-7863-0313-1

Moving Meetings
ISBN   0-7863-0333-6

Multicultural Customer Service
ISBN   0-7863-0332-8